DOES GOD ANSWER PRAYER?

BY JAN MACPHERSON BENNETT

WORD PRODUCTIONS

DEDICATION

"I dedicate this book to the glory of God!"

—Jan Macpherson Bennett

Does God Answer Prayer?
By Jan Macpherson Bennett

Copyright © 2020
By Jan Macpherson Bennett

ISBN: 978-1-7356273-0-4

WORD PRODUCTIONS LLC
PO Box 11185, Albuquerque, NM 87192
www.wordproductions.org

CONTENTS

CHAPTER	PAGE
1. The Phone Conversation	1
2. Praying for a Daughter	5
3. The Girl Trip	7
4. Out-Give God?	9
5. God Can Heal Anyone!	11
6. The Silver Tray	13
7. Praying for a Child	19
8. The House Church	25
9. From Darkness to Light	29
10. Beauty In Flight	31
11. God Will Lead Us	35
12. He Is A Healer	39
13. Our Pot of Gold!	41
14. Our Time Is Short!	43
15. Prayer Scriptures	47

THE PHONE CONVERSATION

And this is the confidence that we have toward him, that if we ask anything according to his will he hears us. And if we know that he hears us in whatever we ask, we know that we have the requests that we have asked of him. —1 John 5:14–15

DOES GOD HEAR OUR PRAYERS? I found out the answer to that after I had been married for twenty-one years and had two teenagers. To show you what I'm talking about, I'm going to tell you some stories.

A retail major at a University in the West, was hired full-time by Macy's in New York City, in the Fall of 2008—after being an intern the summer before. Her family was so excited for her.

She secured two roommates from on-line web sites and from friends-of-friends. They rented a fourth floor, walk-up, three bedroom apartment. One bedroom had an outside street view window—the rest of the apartment only had window well shafts for outside air. The rooms were dark and without a source of light. There was a small bathroom in the apartment.

At first things went fairly smoothly; then one of the roommates started to invite a variety of boyfriends over. Together with her boyfriend, they would take a shower together and then walk around the apartment in only towels.

The girl that was a retail major was hired to be in a management trainee position at Macy's. In spite of that, and because of the financial crisis of 2008, instead of rotating positions, she was stuck behind a computer for eight to ten hours a day learning how to order large quantities of merchandise, such as accessories, among other things.

The employees were required to work longer than eight hours a day. If her job wasn't completed, she was sometimes sitting behind a computer for ten hours a day. She had only one day off for Christmas.

As the new year began, she became increasingly exhausted and stressed by the long hours with so few days off.

Besides the stress at work, she couldn't fully relax at home in her apartment. Before her year lease was up, she decided she couldn't stay in this situation with a variety of men wandering around in towels—and roommates who were unpleasant.

This desire for a new apartment was turned into prayer requests on a 3 x 5 file card. She turned her worries into a prayer! This was in July 2009 that she asked God for exactly what she needed and wanted:

The 3 x 5 Prayer Card Requests
1. *Please help me find a beautiful apartment.*
2. *Please let it have a heavenly atmosphere and be full of light.*
3. *Please let there be a doorman for safety.*
4. *Please let there be an elevator.*
5. *Please let it be in a safe neighborhood.*
6. *Please let it be affordable.*

As you can guess, finding an apartment in New York City is very difficult. Many people pay an agent to help them locate an apartment. The search began before her year lease was up, but time was running out. She wanted to live alone which was also more expensive. From New York City, she called home because she was discouraged.

Her mother said, "Let's go over exactly what we're looking for in an apartment: tell me again, so I can pray."

The Mysterious Lady

As she was riding the bus and on the phone with her mom, she repeated to her exactly what she wanted. As she was talking, a well-dressed lady on the bus handed her a business card and said, "I want to talk to you."

When she finished her phone conversation, the lady said: "I have an apartment that fits the description of what you are looking for. If you are interested I will show it to you."

An appointment was soon made to see the apartment. It was on the 29th floor with many large windows facing east toward Central Park, which was two blocks away.

The 24/7 doormen in the lobby were courteous when she arrived and she admired the very large bouquet of fresh flowers in the lobby.

Quickly renting the apartment, she moved in the day her lease was up on the fourth floor walk-up.

Later, the owner of the apartment explained a few things. She said she very rarely ever rode the bus. She overheard the phone conversation and noticed what a beautiful and stylish young woman she was. She said she had a mid-school aged daughter, and they lived next door to the apartment she was renting.

She thought perhaps her only child would enjoy an inspirational older friend. The price was high, but reasonable for what it offered. It was on 67th near Broadway, two blocks from Lincoln Center, Julliard, and the Metropolitan Opera. This beautiful apartment became home from 2009 to 2015.

You can't out-give the Lord!

PRAYING FOR A DAUGHTER

And this is the confidence that we have toward him, that if we ask anything according to his will he hears us. And if we know that he hears us in whatever we ask, we know that we have the requests that we have asked of him. —1 John 5:14–15

OUR DAUGHTER BROOKE and her husband Taylor had their son Corin, and four years later they had their son Ari. Brooke had a few miscarriages between the boys. They then decided that they wanted to adopt a daughter. We all started praying for a baby girl in the Fall of 2006.

2006: 3 x 5 Prayer Card
Please let the baby be: intelligent, attractive, loving, responsive, healthy, happy, a good sister, a happy family member, one of Your children. Please let all caregivers give her great love until we get her.

2008: 3 x 5 Prayer Card
Thank You for another family member.

2009:   3 x 5 Prayer Card
Please help her mother make wise choices during her pregnancy. Please let the baby feel great love from us and from her mother from

conception. Let us be a blessing to the baby and let the baby be a blessing to us.

In September of 2009, Brooke and Taylor were notified of a baby girl who was one month old, weighing five pounds, who was born in Ethiopia.

Brooke, Taylor, Corin, and Ari went to pick up "Elaia" in Ethiopia on February 12, 2010. They had requested to meet the birth mother if possible. When they were at the orphanage, and while they were picking up Elaia, they met the birth mother. They asked her: "Would you like to meet Elaia's brothers?"

The birth mother was astounded and so happy that Elaia would have brothers. The boys had been off playing. When they came over to meet her, she gave them both a big kiss. While they were in Ethiopia, the entire family flew to a famous Christian church in Axum where all of the women wear white shawls. Brooke took a white shawl for the occasion.

As she was walking toward the church wearing her white shawl and carrying Elaia, a women stopped her and said, "You will be a good mother." That was a blessing to Brooke. Brooke was so happy.

You can't out-give the Lord!

THE GIRL TRIP

And this is the confidence that we have toward him, that if we ask anything according to his will he hears us. And if we know that he hears us in whatever we ask, we know that we have the requests that we have asked of him. —1 John 5:14–15

IN 2014 I HAD A GIRL TRIP with my daughter Brooke, and her daughter, my granddaughter Elaia. We were invited to visit friends in New Haven, Connecticut who were attending Yale University.

On the trip, we took the train down to New York City for one night for two days of sight-seeing. Toward the end of the week-long trip Brooke and I took a walk through the beautiful Yale campus. It was breathtakingly beautiful.

Brooke said, "Mom, I still sort of want to be a doctor."

I said, " I know Brooke, you've wanted to be a doctor since you finished college. But, love came first, marriage, and then children." I continued, " I'll tell you something Brooke, if you want to get into medical school you must be accepted by age 40 or it's too late."

She said , "Really?" Right away I answered, "Yes, absolutely."

Brooke was 38 years old with three children, and a husband. In spite of that, a fire of desire and determination was set in her that day. She began to get all of the course work needed to apply to medical school.

Brooke had watched the University of Texas medical school building being constructed—a fifteen minute drive from her home in Austin, Texas for more than a year by then.

She finished the needed course work, filled out all the applications, and then had the required interviews. There were fifty slots available for this brand new med school class in Austin, Texas.

The first admissions would be announced in December of 2015, and the classes would start in June of 2016. She wasn't admitted but she was on the wait list. We prayed.

Brooke, January 2015: 3 x 5 Prayer Card:
1. *Please guide Brooke's life.*
2. *Please let Your will for Brooke's life be known.*
3. *Please stay with Brooke through this process and please give her guidance.*

Months went by. Brooke went to an open house for the new medical school and heard the new Dean of the medical school speak.

Time went by, and in April she was admitted. During her four years at medical school she served as Co-President of her class. She finished her schooling and started her residency at the University of Texas in Austin, in Primary Care Internal Medicine in the summer of 2020. Brooke and her family are thriving and surviving in new ways with this change in their lives.

You can't out-give the Lord!

Out-Give God?

And this is the confidence that we have toward him, that if we ask anything according to his will he hears us. And if we know that he hears us in whatever we ask, we know that we have the requests that we have asked of him. —1 John 5:14–15

ONCE OUR DAUGHTER Brooke was admitted to medical school, she had to make plans for the family—she had been a stay-at-home-mom for 19 years. Her oldest son would be starting MIT in the Fall in Boston; her second son would be starting LASA High School in Austin; and her six-year-old daughter, Elaia, was currently in first grade and would be starting second grade at Lee Elementary in Austin.

Brooke had heard that there was some sort of child care at Elaia's school but she had never looked into it. She visited the school office and said, "I know there is some type of child care program available at Lee, could you tell me about it?"

The office secretary said, "Oh, we have child care here but everyone signs up their kids at the beginning of kindergarten; there is never any room. However, very unusually, we just happen to have two openings and Elaia can start next year.

And once Elaia is in child care she can stay for the rest of grade school—for the next four years. The fee includes before and after school care, snacks, plus care on school in-service days when the other children don't come to school."

Although Elaia switched to a private school after two years in this program, it was a true blessing for the family.

You can't out-give the Lord!

GOD CAN HEAL ANYONE!

And this is the confidence that we have toward him, that if we ask anything according to his will he hears us. And if we know that he hears us in whatever we ask, we know that we have the requests that we have asked of him. —1 John 5:14–15

I FIRST UNDERSTOOD THE HEALING power of the Lord in answer to prayer, when I was in Bible Study Fellowship many years ago. We were in groups of fifteen to twenty women and we prayed for each other weekly.

My husband had been having a very sore ankle for quite a while and he was wearing a boot from the doctor for support.

We had taken a trip to Europe with our children and he had worn the boot on our trip.

I had the same prayer request all year, "Please heal Dave's ankle completely without surgery."

Dave wore that boot all winter, and by late Spring, after a full winter of prayer from my Bible study friends, he took off the boot and walked normally. He never knew we were praying for him, I never told him. I then realized that you can pray for someone's healing and they do not have to participate. He was healed.

You can't out-give the Lord!

6

THE SILVER TRAY

And this is the confidence that we have toward him, that if we ask anything according to his will he hears us. And if we know that he hears us in whatever we ask, we know that we have the requests that we have asked of him. —1 John 5:14–15

I'M GOING TO TELL YOU a love story—but like many love stories it had some difficult times.

My husband Dave and I met when we were both on a water ski trip on Memorial Day weekend at a New Mexico lake with a singles ski group. I had been invited to go by a date.

Dave and I were on the same water ski boat, and after skiing we sat on the beach and talked. After a while, he invited me to have a dinner of grilled steak, wine, salad and French bread.

My date for the weekend and I had planned cold beans out of a can, so I told Dave "yes."

He and another friend had planned this special dinner and they both had decided to ask dates to join them, once they got to the lake.

Dinner was delicious and we spent the evening on the beach getting to know one another.

The next day, I took my tent down (borrowed from my dad) and my date loaded it in his car along with his tent and a kayak we had taken which was my dad's.

We drove the three and one-half hours to Albuquerque and my date didn't say one word to me. He dumped me in my parents yard along with the kayak and left.

At the end of the summer I reconnected with Dave at an organ concert at UNM, and we then started dating regularly.

I knew I wanted to marry a very smart and capable man who could do anything. This was Dave. We dated all winter. I was a teacher-leader on a teenage tour of Europe and Russia for six weeks the following June and July. I was crazy about Dave.

He proposed the first night I returned, the last day of July. We were married two weeks later. We had a beautiful, small wedding.

Fortunately, his mother and twin brother and sister were spending the summer with Dave from Rochester, New York, and were in town. His other siblings came as well. My family all lived in Albuquerque.

During the first year of our marriage, I realized that Dave had a temper he couldn't control. I was shocked, astounded, and sad—but I wasn't going to leave Dave because of this. I loved Dave. Life went on; work went on. We had a lot of fun together.

We were enjoying our house, our neighbors, and our life. I went to church every Sunday; Dave went sometimes.

I knew that God prefers for people to stay married and since I was truly in love with Dave, this is what I decided to do. After six years, we had a daughter Brooke, and twenty months later our son Grant.

I taught high school Spanish for five years and sold real estate. After that, I was able to stay home and raise our children.

Dave, a scientist, was always a reliable provider for the family but during the years raising our children we had lots of tension in our home. There was yelling and meanness and I worried about our children.

I made a complete family dinner nightly while our kids were growing up: I would have everything ready and we would wait for Dave. Often he would not call and not be home on time and it was frustrating. When he did get home, he was not pleasant many times: he didn't ask us how our day had gone and he was mean. I loved him! Why? I don't know, and it was beyond my understanding. He was a good dad in a variety of ways—he set down rules, and our children didn't stray.

In my attempt to understand Dave, I discovered that Dave had a very difficult childhood with an alcoholic father. I don't know how he would have turned out without a caring mother. Dave's mother was outstanding. She was mother to their five children and basically raised them herself although they remained married.

I realize that Dave thought of marriage as a longterm commitment. As a child, he couldn't invite children over to play because of his dad—so I don't think he learned how to make good friends and bond as most young children do.

Dave did show our children and me his love by always being supportive of our interests.

Many times, I left to travel with relatives and he always said, "go." He took vacation time on three different occasions to watch our kids while I went on three week trips with my mom to Spain, Israel, and South America. The first time I left, our son was two years old and our daughter was four. He was very generous with his total support of my travel and he still is.

When he would lose his temper, be mean, or disappoint me and our children, I would say to him, "Dave, God gave you a wife who will love you no matter what you do."

I truly have loved Dave no matter what...and I still do! To me it's beyond human understanding. But, I do know that it is real! God works in mysterious ways.

I can say that it is a blessing to truly love your husband no matter what. I say this because many people have not been blessed with this type of love.

My children and I have been praying for Dave for years. As Christian believers we pray that Dave will be one also. We pray that he will start to demonstrate the fruits of the spirit (Galatians 5:22-23), love, joy, peace, patience, kindness, goodness, faithfulness, gentleness, and self control. The fruits of the spirit are outward signs that the Holy Spirit is present.

As I write, I'm flying from Austin to Dallas to Albuquerque. We are flying into a beautiful orange-red sunset; the colors are surrounding us. The light misty clouds are filled with colors —pink, orange, yellow—totally surrounding the plane and are touching the wings. We are flying through an orange, cloudy, misty sky. We look through the orange light-filled clouds as they blow by...it's beyond beautiful! It doesn't seem real—a soft orange-pink bank of clouds out the window, and lots of misty orange clouds between us and the ground. The small lakes below reflect a pink and green light: God's artwork.

As I sit here, I reflect that God gave me this intense love for Dave. We have been through a lot during our 50 years of marriage. I believe that people stay married because they decide to stay married; they are committed to each other. It has been an extreme challenge, and at the same time an extreme pleasure that is hard to explain and hard to understand.

Back to God hearing our prayers! After twenty-one years of marriage, we had been in our new house for one year and things were not going well.

Dave and I were bringing out the worst in each other. He was sick of me and I was sick of him. I could tell he was giving up. We had hit a brick wall—He was on one side and I was on the other. There was no way around it.

I called up my sister and said "Our marriage is over—I can feel it—what can I do?"

She said, "I'll be right over." She told me to read the first 50 pages of *The Christian Secret of a Happy Life* by Hannah Whitehall Smith and left saying, "I'll be praying for you."

From this book, I learned that I needed to turn this situation over to the Lord. By faith in God, I needed to visualize our broken and failing marriage as a gift-package that I was placing on a silver tray and giving it totally to the Lord. I was not to hold on to any part of it. I was to turn it totally over to the Lord. Every time I began to think about it and to worry about it I was to place it totally on that silver tray. I was to totally give it to the Lord. Every few seconds I would worry and then say, "Here Lord, this is Yours to handle."

Over and over again for days I did this. Although we were still in the same house, things were bad. Over and over again I handed it over. Our children were in high school. At this point, they had sensed and felt the conflict and tension in our house forever. I just kept praying and handing it over. My sister kept praying and very slowly I could sense things were improving.

It was slow. My sister and I never quit praying. I kept handing it over to the Lord. Our marriage got back on an even keel. Our marriage didn't dissolve.

During this time, right before we hit the brick wall, I walked out the door and told Grant, "I'm going to talk to a lawyer about a divorce." He said, "Don't, I want a dad." That was almost thirty years ago.

After learning how to turn our marriage in its very broken state over to the Lord, for the first time I really knew that God hears our prayers. He heard my prayers and accepted my broken gift on a silver tray. He took that broken gift I gave to him and He began to mend and heal it.

Marriage is not just for us; it's for our children and our grandchildren. There is stability, a family home, the security of parents who are still together, the extended family gatherings. It's for the couple to be there for each other—to be companions, helpmates, lovers, and nursemaids when needed. Marriage is very difficult; it's also very wonderful. It's a complicated package.

In my longterm marriage, I watch us get weaker, more feeble, less able to do things, and it's sobering. I am thankful to have someone in my life, in my house, and in my bed. God provided this for me out of His love. He answered my prayer. I believe that humans are meant for relationships that last, and we all long for them. Without God's intervention there isn't much hope. I have seen God answer my prayers! With His help, we are still married.

You can't out-give the Lord!

Praying for a Child

And this is the confidence that we have toward him, that if we ask anything according to his will he hears us. And if we know that he hears us in whatever we ask, we know that we have the requests that we have asked of him. —1 John 5:14–15

OUR SON GRANT WENT to Colorado State University and majored in civil engineering. He loved CSU from the very first day. He was very involved in student government. When he graduated in 2000, I invited him to go on a five-week train trip through northern Spain, southern France, Monaco, and Italy. My husband Dave joined us for two weeks in Monaco and Italy.

After Grant had worked as a civil engineer in Denver for four years, I invited him to join me and my cousin on a trip to India and Bhutan in the Himalayas. He was able to arrange a three week vacation to go with us on this adventure.

After our trip, he continued working as a civil engineer for two more years and then became a PE (a professional engineer).

About this time he met Barbara, a beautiful girl who had also grown up in Albuquerque. They met on a week long bicycle adventure arranged by their church. Grant had recently bought an old house in downtown Denver.

After our trip I started praying. Below are prayer cards from my prayer card files. The dates show that we prayed for Grant's eventual marriage for five years before he married. He was covered in prayer!

Himalaya trip 6-31-2004:
Praise for a perfect trip to the Himalayas with full protection— Thank You.

10-18-2004:
That You will give Grant a fabulous social life of Your perfect timing and Your perfect design.

10-31-2004:
Thank you for drawing Grant closer to You. Please continue to draw him to You. Please bring forth the perfect woman of Your choosing for Grant—one of Yours—his perfect companion.

1-12-2006:
Please let Grant have a blast of a social life with high quality, worthy people—a wonderful social life of Your perfect timing and Your perfect design that is incredibly fun, with quality and enriching activities.

7-21-06:
Praise for Grant's good health, loving kindness, enthusiasm for all of life. Please guide him to the woman of Your choosing when the time is right.

5-30-2007:

Praise for Grant's friendship with Barbara. Please bless this relationship if it is Your will to do so.

6-18-2007:

Praise for the friendship of Barbara and Grant. If this relationship is Your perfect will for both of them, please let their relationship continue to grow beautifully. Let them experience incredible joy and happiness. If it is Your will, please let them get married and have a fabulous lifetime partnership.

8-20-2007:

Please let the courtship cross over into engagement and then marriage with Your perfect timing.

9-10-2007:

Thank You for letting Grant survive the crash with a car on his skateboard four days ago. Please let him heal completely. Please let him to be more cautious in traffic. Please guide Grant's activities and life.

12-9-07:

Praise for Grant and Barbara's wonderful trip to Brazil. Praise for their happiness, their safety, and their relationship. Please continue to guide this relationship.

5-1-2008:

If it is Your will that Grant and Barbara get married, please let them fall deeply in love with each other and desire this. Please let them recognize the unique qualities in each other that makes this so right.

Especially let Grant:
—Let him pursue Barbara with zeal
—Recognize in Barbara: her intelligence, their similar interests, her darling looks, her incredible interest in his health, diabetes, lifestyle and needs.
—Do not let Barbara slip out of his life for lack of attention.
—Let him recognize and appreciate her incredible qualities and love her deeply and vice versa.
—Please bless Barbara's desire to get a master's degree and let it work into their relationship. Please help her easily afford it.

8-31-2008:
Praise for Grant's: financial success; good health; handsomeness; love of You; and his desire to be a good son.

2-2-2009:
Praise to You for the engagement of Grant and Barbara. Please guide them at all times as they prepare for their marriage. Please bless their love and friendship. Please let the location of their wedding be of Your perfect will. Please guide the family on how to put together a meaningful and wonderful wedding and reception that is within our means and brings joy to all.

4-6-2009:
Please help Barbara do very well at her job interviews. Please help her get the perfect job for her in the perfect location. Praise for Barbara's Masters Degree in such a short time.

5-21-2009:

Please let the shower for Barbara be: fun, festive, filled with love.
Please let the food be delicious.
Please let everyone be rested and maintain their energy; especially those in the wedding so everyone can have a blast.
Please let the whole event be a total joy.

7-7-2009:

Please guide all activities the month surrounding the wedding. Please make the wedding ceremony special and a blessing to all who attend, and let it go perfectly. Please bless the reception including the food, flowers, guests, and bride and groom. Please guide every part of the rehearsal dinner.

Answer to the Prayers

Grant and Barbara were married on September 6, 2009. We learned at the wedding that Barbara's family had also been praying for her eventual marriage and happiness. They have now been married for eleven years. They had a long courtship covered in prayer. Now they are very busy juggling two full time careers, plus their four year old daughter Emmaline, and their nine month old daughter Annalise.

As we live our lives and continually pray we know that…

You can't out-give the Lord!

8

THE HOUSE CHURCH

And this is the confidence that we have toward him, that if we ask anything according to his will he hears us. And if we know that he hears us in whatever we ask, we know that we have the requests that we have asked of him. —1 John 5:14–15

IN 2006, OUR DAUGHTER Brooke, and Taylor her husband, decided to move from their comfortable home in north Austin, Texas to inner city Austin and start a house-church with a group of their friends.

They located a very small lot in their price range which had an old shack on it in East Austin. They made an offer to buy the lot. Soon, they found out there was an illegal lien on the lot. Austin had recently passed a McMansion rule that you couldn't build a home that was disproportionately tall compared to the lot. The law was set to go into effect very close to when their building plans needed to be approved by the city. They couldn't build a house big enough for their family if they couldn't go up three stories. There was a noontime cut off for the rule to go into effect. We started to pray. Here is how we prayed:

1. Please guide the plans for the house.
2. Please help the plans be approved before the deadline.

They heard no reply from the lot owner on their offer by the day the McMansion law was going into effect.

Brooke was at home in north Austin, and Taylor was working at home. Brooke wasn't even going to try to get a building permit before the deadline at noon. She thought it was hopeless.

Taylor said, "If you don't try we'll never know, let's see what God will do today."

So Brooke took their four and a-half-year-old son, Ari, and a few toys, and went to City Hall which was a thirty minute drive away. She went into the office and up to the permit window.

The lady handed her a large stack of papers that had to be turned in by the noon deadline. Brooke looked at the clock on the wall. It was 10:00 AM. She thought to herself, "What am I doing here? This is impossible."

She had to turn in a survey of the lot with the basic house plans drawn out. She had the current survey with the current house (shack) drawn on it.

The copy machine at City Hall only took change—she didn't have any. She drove to the nearby library, and that copy machine also took change, and she only had a credit card! She drove back to City Hall. What was she going to do?

She finally talked to a kind clerk in the city copying office. This clerk helped her. She gave her some white out and Brooke whited-out the shack plans and all the specifications for the shack off of the survey that she had.

She then drew the basic house plans for the new house on this survey. The clerk made copies for Brooke for free.

Next Brooke called Taylor and said, "I need to turn in complete electrical specifications and plans."

A prominent Austin contractor who happened to be there, overheard her phone conversation and said, "I can do that for you. Tell me about your house plans."

He then completely filled out the necessary paperwork. Brooke went back to the clerk at the permit window to turn in the paperwork.

The clerk said, "You still need a permit for a water tap. You need to go downstairs to get that. I'll put your name on the list but I can't take your paperwork until it's all complete."

The clock was ticking. Brooke went downstairs with her son and his toys. The water tap permit office was still open, and thankfully they hadn't yet closed for lunch.

Brooke got the necessary stamp on the water permit, and then went back up to the building permit office.

The lady at the window said, "I'm sorry, we're not taking any more permits for houses, the deadline had passed." Brooke said, "Remember, you wrote my name on the list and I went downstairs to get the water tap permit."

The lady said, "Oh yes, I remember. I already put my list away, let me go find it." Then she said, "Yes, your name is here, give me your stack of papers." That was a miracle!

Brooke handed them over, the clerk rolled them up together, put them with the other rolled up permit papers, and said, "You'll be hearing from us." Brooke had seen God moving on her behalf.

Meanwhile, the Realtor and the lot owner had succeeded in having the lien removed from the lot they wanted to buy.

Taylor and their seven year old son Corin met Brooke and Ari at the title company. They closed on the lot at 2:30 PM that same afternoon.

After they bought the lot, they tore down the shack with their church friends using a small front-end loader. They found needles everywhere in the shack and on the ground along with safety kits for prostitutes.

Brooke became the general contractor for their new house. They hired an architect to help design the house. The house was finished in 2007 and they have lived there since then.

You can't out-give the Lord!

From Darkness to Light

And this is the confidence that we have toward him, that if we ask anything according to his will he hears us. And if we know that he hears us in whatever we ask, we know that we have the requests that we have asked of him. —1 John 5:14–15

AS THEY WERE BUILDING the house, I was given an assignment to stain long thin slats that would be used in the living room ceiling. I worked in the front yard where the slats were hung between saw horses. As I worked for a few days in a row, I saw cars pull up next door, someone would get out, go up to the door quickly, come back to the car and leave. This went on all day long every day.

I said to Brooke, "You have drug dealers next door." The house had many people living in it, apparently all relatives.

Eventually Brooke befriended the elderly mother Victoria, who only spoke Spanish. She was a sister of the owner. Brooke had her over for tea and vice-versa.

As time went on, the drug dealing continued, and the various relatives squeezed Victoria from a nice suite in the house to a small bedroom.

One day, while Brooke and Victoria were having tea, Victoria said, "If we ever want to sell our house, would you like to make an offer on it?"

Eventually, the various relatives moved Victoria into a nursing home out of Austin. The drug business was flourishing.

On one of my visits to Austin, a friend from church who knew the situation said, "Pray that the darkness next door will be overcome with light, and that Brooke's family will be kept safe during the process."

I really liked this idea so I started praying this. The darkness continued in the house. Victoria was not there. One day, Victoria came back for a visit and Brooke invited her over. She said they had decided to sell the house. Brooke had also been notified of this by an e-mail sent by the owner, Victoria's sister. She remembered that Brooke was possibly interested in it.

In the email she began, "The relatives will have a chance to buy the house first." She offered to sell the house to any of the relatives living there or to Brooke and Taylor.

When none of the relatives came forward to buy it, Brooke and Taylor made an offer and they settled on a price.

The darkness was dissolved (no police raid) and all of the relatives left.

Brooke became the general contractor, and the house was totally gutted down to the studs—it was updated and renovated. They now have a unique rental property next to them and only God knows all the ways prayers will be answered there.

You can't out-give the Lord!

Beauty In Flight

And this is the confidence that we have toward him, that if we ask anything according to his will he hears us. And if we know that he hears us in whatever we ask, we know that we have the requests that we have asked of him. —1 John 5:14–15

AS I CONTINUE TO RECOGNIZE how God has moved in my life, I want to recount the following experience:

"I am once again on a plane looking down from my window seat. Flying to Kansas City and then to Austin. Taylor is going skiing in Colorado with all of the Texas friends and our son Grant from Denver will be with them—a boy trip. I am helping run the house while Taylor is away. Brooke is working in the emergency room this week and will have a few overnight shifts. I will get Ari and Elaia to school, help make breakfast, and keep the house going. I have been praying for energy, strength and guidance. I am no longer a "spring chicken." I have never flown to Kansas City to get to Austin.

I am sitting on the north side of the plane so I do not have the hot sun coming in the window. I have card files with answered prayer cards with me. Our flight is almost empty —I have the luxury of a whole row of seats to myself. The flight continues from Kansas City to Austin—it's a total of four hours flying time. I bought a red chile and bacon breakfast burrito at "Tia Juanita's" at the Albuquerque airport—a favorite with flight crews. After I got my burrito and tucked it in my backpack for lunch, I heard them say they ran out of eggs! The flight crews waiting to buy breakfast were amazed and disappointed. Glad I got mine! I am enjoying peanuts and hot tea and looking at beautiful cloud formations out the window.

At home I have been noticing the beauty of God's creations. Brooke sent me an Orchid for Mother's Day, which came in the mail from Amazon! It came in a tall box, with a long green garden stick in the pot to keep it from being crushed. It did lose a few flowers in transport but was still very beautiful. Now it's blooming again seven months later. I've noticed that making Orchid flowers is a slow process—they start on a green stem and then slowly grow, develop, and open. When you watch, you realize it is a labor of love from our Creator.

My house is full of Cyclamens, my favorite flower. I am overwhelmed by the various color combinations—so creative; so beautiful; so heavenly. I love watching them bloom—also a slow process. I love Cyclamens because they are dramatic. When they are thirsty, they totally droop and when you soak them they perk right up. Also, their flowers move around and change positions. House flowers are my delight. Fortunately, we have beautiful windows facing south with lots of light in our house. The plants love it and so do we.

I'm seeing a partially frozen lake as we approach Kansas City, a large, meandering river, and contoured fields ready for crops and a few large farm houses. I love it when we have a smooth landing like we just did—good pilot!

We landed 30 minutes early—plenty of time to eat my packed burrito lunch while I stay on the same plane.

We are now headed to Austin. When I look down I see a large blanket of clouds—they look just like a blanket of cotton balls. Once in a while I can see fields below them. From here, the horizon is bright blue, but leaving Kansas City the sky was very hazy. This blue sky looks like our typical New Mexico sky. I have a whole row of seats to myself again—what luxury!

Approaching Austin, we are now going down through the clouds. White clouds above, beside, below; sunlight streaming in; now totally cloudy; no view; now between clouds above and clouds below descending into Austin. Sun on clouds above—sun on clouds below. Cloud shadows on clouds below, from clouds above. We are in a world of clouds. All I can see are clouds—up, down, and in the distance.

The upturned Southwest Airlines wing is out my left window. I'm just in front of the engine, in row six. No visibility as we are landing—almost down now. Now I see land through fog.

Very smooth landing again. The miracle of flight!

So glad to be spending a week in Austin. The beautiful blessing of family. God continually blesses us with beauty all around us—we just have to train our eyes to see it. He also continually blesses us with other people, friends and family, and those we don't know. We need to realize the people in our lives are another blessing from God.

You can't out-give the Lord!

11

GOD WILL LEAD US

And this is the confidence that we have toward him, that if we ask anything according to his will he hears us. And if we know that he hears us in whatever we ask, we know that we have the requests that we have asked of him. —1 John 5:14–15

WE RAISED OUR CHILDREN in a great neighborhood with a swim team, golf and tennis lessons, and the country club a short bike ride away. There were lots of great friends everywhere. It was close to Dave's work.

When Brooke was an eighth-grader she started acting like something was wrong. I said, "Brooke what's wrong?" She said, "The gang girls are threatening to beat me up after school; they have been doing it for a few days."

Our children were going to a tough middle school, but we were not focusing on it. Brooke was already an eighth-grader and Grant was a sixth-grader. Many of our neighbor's children went to the same school.

The next day, I talked to the school vice-principal and asked, "Can you guarantee Brooke's safety at this school?" He said, "No. Everywhere she goes she needs to have a friend with her, including going to her locker, the bathroom, or to the barracks."

I said, "This is my children's last day at this school." This started a long process of building a new home in an excellent school district and moving. Our children began in a new school the next day.

We have always had rental property in our family. Once we moved, we then started renting our former home. Years went by. Dave decided to update our former home so that we could eventually move back into it. More years went by. The remodel was stalled. Meanwhile I had been watering the very large yard full of tall beautiful pine trees and juniper bushes. I had been watering this very large corner lot for forty-seven years, our whole married life, even when we had tenants.

We live in a desert, and trees die without frequent water. After quite a few years, as I watered, I would notice pieces of asphalt roof tiles in the yard. There can be stiff breezes through his neighborhood from a nearby mountain canyon which had blown down the roof tiles. They were also getting brittle with age.

Repairs and renovations were stalled. I knew God had a plan for this property but the long struggle to watch the house partially renovated for years was very, very difficult. Many, many, prayers had been sent up for guidance.

In April of 2017, I was watering and again noticed more roof tiles in the yard.

The Lord said to me in my mind: "Sell the house now."

I went home and told Dave, "We are going to sell our house now."

He answered, "I don't have time, I'm too busy."

I said, "No, we are going to sell our house now."

He said, "I don't know what it's worth."

I said, "I do." (My references gave me a good idea).

He said, "I don't know how to find a buyer."

I said, "I do."

I went to "We Pay Cash for Houses" on the Internet. We got two bids for cash and accepted the higher one. Our house was sold and closed within two months.

The cash buyers totally updated the house inside and out. They made it extremely attractive. They resold the updated house within four months of their purchase at the very top of the current market value. They made a good profit on their purchase because they were able to buy it from us for a reasonable price. The neighbors were happy with the beautiful new update, the new owners were happy, and we were happy that our family home had a new beginning and a new life.

You can't out-give the Lord!

12

CHAPTER

HE IS A HEALER

And this is the confidence that we have toward him, that if we ask anything according to his will he hears us. And if we know that he hears us in whatever we ask, we know that we have the requests that we have asked of him. —1 John 5:14–15

DOES GOD HEAR OUR PRAYERS? I am now in my mid-seventies. I have now lived longer than both of my parents by five years. Since I turned seventy, I have been feeling my age.

My younger brother, Richard (12 years younger), and I planned a trip to Spain in October of 2017. Right before the trip I wrenched my knee and it was very painful to walk.

My sister Mary and I always write prayer cards before every trip. We pray for continual guidance, good health, and safety.

I took my husband's cane with me just in case (he had a double knee replacement five years earlier). I actually used the cane for four days.

The trip was a demanding one—bags in the hall by 6:45 AM, breakfast from 7:00-8:00 AM; and board the bus by 8:15 AM.

We saw everything! We walked for miles in all the fascinating medieval sections of Madrid, and the Spanish cities in Andalusia and Catalonia. The local guides leading our tours rarely stopped—they just kept walking at a slow pace.

Our tour was large, we had forty-one people in it, and we were all strung out as we walked. We wore "whispers" around our necks to hear the guide.

Photography is my passion. If I stopped to take a photo, the tour kept going and I would lose them. We actually lost a tour member for one hour who stopped and took a photo, and lost track of our group.

Between my sore knee and the fast guides, I got very few pictures, compared to my five other trips to Spain. I prayed for strength to keep up; I prayed for strength to keep going.

Rich was a great companion. My knee was still healing six months after the trip.

My prayers to keep up were answered, sore knee and all. Will I be able to travel abroad again I wondered? I have been able to continue to play tennis. Praise God. I know that God has a plan for my last years. I know that...

You can't out-give the Lord!

13

CHAPTER

OUR POT OF GOLD!

And this is the confidence that we have toward him, that if we ask anything according to his will he hears us. And if we know that he hears us in whatever we ask, we know that we have the requests that we have asked of him. —1 John 5:14–15

I'VE BEEN WRITING PRAYER cards with my sister, Mary, for at least 20 years.

I recently found a prayer card written for my grandson, Corin, who has now graduated from MIT in Boston and he is in graduate school at Harvard. On the card, I prayed that Corin would learn to crawl. These prayers, and the cards have become so precious to me.

When should you write a prayer card? If anything is worrying you, turn the worry into a prayer and write the prayer down on a prayer card:

Put the name of the person or the subject on the upper left side of a 3 x 5 card, and on the upper right hand side, the date you write the prayer card.

Once the prayer is written, add it to your other prayer cards. Pray through the cards when you can, daily, weekly, monthly—it's up to you.

We have prayed for twenty years, and more for some things, Once a prayer has been answered, we write "Thank You," or "Praise and Thanks" on the card, with the date—then we file the card away for safe-keeping.

This is our pot of gold—our hundreds of prayers that have been answered. It is not until you start writing down prayers and saving them that you realize when your prayers are answered.

When looking through my prayer cards, I'm often surprised when I realize, "Oh, that prayer has been answered...I forgot that I wrote down that prayer."

Some prayers can be prayed for many, many years before they are answered. God's timing is not man's timing. We must learn to be patient and have faith and understand that God is in control. This is not always easy to do. The Lord has a plan for our lives, and we must remember that...

You can't out-give the Lord!

OUR TIME IS SHORT

And this is the confidence that we have toward him, that if we ask anything according to his will he hears us. And if we know that he hears us in whatever we ask, we know that we have the requests that we have asked of him. —1 John 5:14–15

WHILE WRITING THIS BOOK I have a sense of urgency to write these testimonials down on paper. I realize my time on earth is running out, and I cannot do this when I'm gone.

God has been so faithful to hear our prayers over all these years and to answer them. I am so humbled that our Almighty God will listen to our prayers and get involved in our lives.

When I see the images from the Hubble Telescope, I realize that our entire earth is like a speck of dust in the universe we can see, and yet God hears our prayers and gets involved in our lives. It's amazing, miraculous, and wonderful!

I visited the new Museum of the Bible in Washington, DC during a trip. The Museum opened in November of 2017. I was disappointed that the museum didn't show the majesty of God or explain the Bible well. I am not only actually disappointed, but puzzled by this.

To understand the Bible can take a lifetime of study, but if I hadn't studied the Bible I would have understood very little in the museum. The museum missed the opportunity to better explain our fabulous God. Millions of dollars and good intentions have gone into the museum. Why is it so vague?

There is a popular song that begins with, "Our God is an awesome God." This is so true. Let me continue to recount this trip:

I am 40,000 feet in the air flying from Washington DC to Kansas City, and then to Albuquerque, I was getting my thoughts on paper for this book.

There I was on the plane and one of my favorite things to do is to be up high and look down. I always get a window seat and I always enjoy the view.

A Beautiful Flight

On my long trip flying to Washington, DC from Albuquerque, I write these desriptions:

I can see towns;

I can see roads; large rivers; and smaller, meandering streams; lakes; and plots of snow-covered land.

I can see cities,but I can't see cars or people.

I can barely see clusters of buildings.

I can get a general view of the layout of a city and the green areas in it.

I can see windows only when they shine in the sun.

I can see the very hazy horizon.

I can see the smoke from factory smoke stacks.

I can see wispy clouds between our plane and earth, almost like a thin veil. Once in a while I can see another plane in the sky.

I flew into DC six days ago, the first of January in 2018. We flew down the Potomac River toward Reagan airport, and the river was frozen. It was really beautiful. The east coast had just been through a severe cold snap.

Of course we can't get God's view of things, but looking down from 40,000 feet helps to put the world we live in into perspective

From this vantage point it is humbling to realize how small man is and yet

God hears our prayers.

You can't out-give the Lord!

PRAYER SCRIPTURES

And my God will supply every need of yours according to his riches in glory in Christ Jesus. —Philippians 4:19

And this is the confidence that we have toward him, that if we ask anything according to his will he hears us. —1 John 3:13-14

Do not be anxious about anything, but in everything by prayer and supplication with thanksgiving let your requests be made known to God. And the peace of God, which surpasses all understanding, will guard your hearts and your minds in Christ Jesus.
—Philippians 4:6-7

The word of the Lord came to Jeremiah: "Behold, I am the Lord, the God of all flesh. Is anything too hard for me? —Jeremiah 32:27

"Remember not the former things, nor consider the things of old. Behold, I am doing a new thing; now it springs forth, do you not perceive it? I will make a way in the wilderness and rivers in the desert.
—Isaiah 43:18-19

Now to him who is able to do far more abundantly than all that we ask or think, according to the power at work within us, to him be glory in the church and in Christ Jesus throughout all generations, forever and ever. Amen.
—Ephesians 3:20-21

And I am sure of this, that he who began a good work in you will bring it to completion at the day of Jesus Christ. —Philippians 1:6

In that day you will ask nothing of me. Truly, truly, I say to you, whatever you ask of the Father in my name, he will give it to you. Until now you have asked nothing in my name. Ask, and you will receive, that your joy may be full. —John 16:23–24

And this is the confidence that we have toward him, that if we ask anything according to his will he hears us. And if we know that he hears us in whatever we ask, we know that we have the requests that we have asked of him. —1 John 5:14–15

Whatever you ask in my name, this I will do, that the Father may be glorified in the Son. If you ask me anything in my name, I will do it. —John 14:13–14

For all the promises of God find their Yes in him. That is why it is through him that we utter our Amen to God for his glory. —2 Corinthians 1:20

MY NOTES

_____

_____

_____

_____

_____

_____

_____

_____

_____

_____

_____

_____

_____

_____

_____

_____

_____

_____

_____

_____

_____

_____

_____

_____

_____

_____

_____

_____

_____

_____

_____

_____

_____

_____

_____

_____

_____

_____

_____

_____

_____

_____

_____

_____

_____

_____

_____

_____

_____

_____

_____

_____

_____

_____

_____

_____

_____

_____

_____

_____

_____

_____

_____

_____

_____

_____

_____

_____

_____

_____

_____

_____

_____

_____

_____

_____

_____

_____

_____

www.ingramcontent.com/pod-product-compliance
Lightning Source LLC
Chambersburg PA
CBHW071853020426
42331CB00007B/1981